LET'S EXPLORE CANADA
(MOST FAMOUS ATTRACTIONS IN CANADA)

Speedy Publishing LLC
40 E. Main St. #1156
Newark, DE 19711
www.speedypublishing.com

Copyright 2018

Canada is a country in the northern part of the continent of North America. Canada is a developed country and one of the wealthiest in the world.

Niagara Falls
are made up of
3 waterfalls, the
American Falls,
the Bridal Veil Falls
and the Horseshoe
Falls. he Niagara
River is about 58
kilometres in length
and is the natural
outlet from Lake Erie
to Lake Ontario.

Banff National Park is Canada's oldest national park. Banff National Park is the most visited Alberta tourist destination and one of the most visited national parks in North America. Banff National Park welcomes between 3-4 million visitors annually.

ROGERS CEN
ROGERS CENTRE

The CN Tower is a 1,815.4 ft-high concrete communications and observation tower in Downtown Toronto. More than 2 million people visit the CN Tower every year.

Whistler Mountain is a Canadian resort town in the southern Pacific Ranges of the Coast Mountains in the province of British Columbia, Canada. Over two million people visit Whistler annually, primarily for alpine skiing and snowboarding.

Parliament Hill is an area of Crown land on the southern banks of the Ottawa River in downtown Ottawa, Ontario. Parliament Hill is the political and cultural heart of the city.

The Bay of Fundy is known for having the highest tidal range in the world. The Bay of Fundy has a diverse ecosystem and a marine biodiversity comparable to the Amazon Rainforest.

Stanley Park is a 1,001-acre public park that borders the downtown of Vancouver in British Columbia, Canada. The park has a long history and was one of the first areas to be explored in the city.